For more than half of a century,
Supposed to be here". We spent ⟨
under the guidance of one of the ⟨
Bishop Samuel M. Crouch. I was friend to her brother, Arthur, who was
transitioned from this world to a world to come all too soon. Looking back
over those years, perhaps, we could have authored the book.

Having read the presentation, I am grateful to Dr. Barbara Bean for allowing
the Holy Spirit to use her in writing her own story. Her book will give guidance, hope and inspiration to a generation of believers with a different per-
spective on Christian living. It is a new breed of believers in search of their
purpose for living and looking to achieve results.

Principle training is key to the proper channeling of their energies and
attaining results. The Testimonies and experience of the author, provides
the avenue for that kind of training. It has been previously noted life is difficult, as it is a hard school master. Because, it gives us first the test and then
we learn the lesson. The lessons here have all been learned by experience.

Through this book, you will find instruction on how to set aside mediocrity
and complacency. It will inspire you to join the special mission of walking a
path in a spiritual realm, that has been experienced by the author.

It is my prayer that this book will become the instrument God uses to
remove spiritual blindness and the tool need by God's people to possess the
land that Jesus conquered through His sacrifice at the cross.

Bishop Harold Edwards
Church Of The Living God
Dallas, Texas

I'm Not Supposed To Be Here

But God

Dr. Barbara Bean

XULON ELITE

Xulon Press Elite
2301 Lucien Way #415
Maitland, FL 32751
407.339.4217
www.xulonpress.com

Paperback ISBN-13: 978-1-6628-7428-4
Ebook ISBN-13: 978-1-6628-7429-1

FOREWORD

C risis comes in all shapes, sizes, and different ages. The author, Dr. Barbara Bean of *I'm Not Supposed To Be Here* takes us on her journey and shares her remarkable story amidst all the conflicting and confusing emotions she experienced during her early impressionable childhood years. Drawing from her experience, Dr Bean is transparent ("authentic self") as she exposes her low self-esteem, feelings of not being good enough, putting a label on her appearance, and making a comparison to her peers which one too many women experience not only in churches, but in our society as a whole today.

She finally came to the realization that from birth, God knew she was supposed to be here. Her story reminded me of the scripture Jeremiah 1:5 (NIV). "Before I formed you in the womb, I knew you; before you were born I set you apart and appointed you."

Today, Evangelist Dr. Barbara Bean is appointed and anointed by God to teach and preach God's Word. She has a clear vision of who she is in the body of Christ and can testify Psalm 139:14 (NIV), which says, "I praise you because I am fearfully and wonderfully made; your works are wonderful; I know full well." Yes, Barbara was different in a good way and set apart as a vessel of honor to be used for God's glory. He is a faithful and an unchanging God against all odds we experience in life.

Dr. Bean is a personal friend dating back to our school days in the late 1950s and early 1960s. In later years, she became a member of the New Antioch Church where my husband, the late Bishop James A. Lewis, pastored for thirty-six years. Now our son, Supt Jeffrey M. Lewis, is pastor. Dr Bean has been a member of New Antioch for more than thirty years. She and her husband, Elder Leslie Bean, are considered to be pillars of the ministry. Her dedicated service to the work of the Lord and valuable experience as an Evangelist missionary as well as her doctoral degree training has contributed greatly to the advancement of the New Antioch Church.

God indeed created this vessel of honor to survive. This is a compelling story of hope against despair; it is a *must-read* book and should be shared with women of every multi-generational, socio-economic, and educational level.

Dr. Barbara McCoo Lewis
General Supervisor–International Department of Women
Jurisdictional Supervisor–Southern California First
Ecclesiastical Jurisdiction
Church of God in Christ, Inc.
Author of
Christian Women's Guide to
Church Protocol and Saintly Decorum

Bean Family

DEDICATION

To my loving husband, Leslie, and my children, Kevin, Karen, Da'Niel, Ola, and Les, Jr. Thank you for your love and understanding. I could not have written this without your support.

To my spiritual leaders, Pastor Jeffrey M. Lewis and First Lady Floetta Lewis, who lead one of the greatest churches, The New Antioch Church of God in Christ, Los Angeles, California. It's because of your continual preaching and teaching us to obey God that we can step out of our comfort zones and not allow intimidation to stop us. As long as you know that God has ordained you, you have His permission to go forth and pursue your purpose.

God has impressed upon me to write about my life growing up. Where I came from, my family, my struggles, and my call to ministry. I've tried to be discreet in being transparent. I'm not at all sure about this, but I can't seem to get away from it. I dedicate these pages to each of you who are hesitant to move forward because of your past, but it should be your past that pushes you to move forward.

TABLE OF CONTENTS

ACKNOWLEDGEMENTS

Thanks be to God who caused me to put pen to paper about my life's struggles, issues, and triumphs.

I would like to thank our general mother of the Churches of God in Christ and jurisdictional supervisor of Southern California, Mother Barbara Mc-Coo Lewis, for seeing in me what I could not see in myself. Thank you Bishop Dad Lewis who taught us "just do it."

To Deacon Terry Owens, thank you for taking time to review and edit this project. Thank all of you who encouraged me to write and complete this book. To God be the glory.

INTRODUCTION

Philippians 1:6 (NIV)

Being confident of this, that he who begun a good work in you will carry it on to completion until the day of Christ Jesus.

This book is written to every man, woman, boy, and girl who has been challenged by the Enemy not to pursue their purpose. You may think that you have done so many things that you are ashamed of and now you feel that God has no use for you. Be reminded in John 10:10, *that the thief (Satan) comes to steal, kill and destroy, but I (Christ) have come that you might have life and that more abundantly.*

Our trials come to make us strong and the things we experience in life help us to inspire other believers that if God can use anything or anybody, we are no exception. It's not always easy to share your downfalls and missteps, but remember you're not alone. Some of the greatest evangelists, pastors, and missionaries have experienced most if not all of the same things.

I used to think that every great preacher lived a spotless life from the time they were born until they accepted the call, and that's why God moves in their ministry so powerfully. But after listening to their testimonies, I was amazed to know how the Enemy tried to trick them, too.

God has dealt with me so patiently to do this assignment, but now there's an urgency to share what pushed me into my purpose.

May God minister to your spirit and encourage you to pursue your purpose with tenacity and boldness knowing that you, too, have the assurance that God is on your side.

Love and prayers.

Chapter 1

WHO KNEW . . . ?

Way down yonder in Kenansville, North Carolina, I was born to Mabel and Arthur Wynn, but who knew what was in store for me?

A few weeks after my birth, my mother passed away. I never had a chance to bond with her. My brother, Arthur Jr., and I were sent from one place to another, from family member to family member, until finally, the orphanage.

My dad had moved to California where jobs were available and he could make enough money for us to come and live with him. Because of the rules and regulations of the South, North Carolina statutes would not allow him to get us unless he was married.

After the death of my mother, he began dating a young lady by the name of Ruby Lee Williams, and after sharing with her about his dilemma, Ruby agreed to marry him so that he could bring his children to California. So at nine months old, my dad and my new mom brought my brother and I to Los Angeles, which has remained our home.

I remember I was a sickly child having diphtheria and whooping cough. Understand that during this time, medical attention for

1

Negroes was not always accessible. Our mom would take us on the trolley to 'Big G' (General Hospital) every day to see a doctor. There were times I thought I would not live to see the age of ten. My body was frail, my eyes were weak, and I felt like I was going to cough my life away, but with the prayers of my dad and mom, they loved me back to health.

I had no idea of what the plan of God was for my life. After all, I was just a child.

One thing I will always remember, I was different from other children. It seemed as though I could never get away with anything. I can remember one time when my mother told me not to go outside in my bedclothes. My brother went outside with his bedclothes on, so I felt I could, too. One day while we were playing on the front porch, our mom came home and found us playing with our bedclothes on, hair uncombed, and no slippers or shoes on. Not only was there a scolding, but a spanking that I will never forget.

At the age of seven, I accepted the Lord as my Savior, and was filled with the Holy Ghost praying on my knees on my eighth birthday.

Shortly after being saved, I had the strangest dream. We lived in a back house, and our front door was a Dutch door. The top part of the door was open, and I saw what looked like a train coming out of the sky. When it got to my door, the conductor asked for my ticket. I saw a lot of the saints singing and praising God on the train, and as I handed the conductor my ticket, I woke up.

Then a voice spoke so clearly in my ears saying, '*And other sheep I have, which are not of this fold, them also I must bring, and they shall hear my voice, and there shall be one-fold and one shepherd.*'

I am not a dreamer; however, for me to remember what I had dreamed, there must be something to it. It wasn't until years later that I found out that the voice in my dream had recited a scripture from the Bible, John 10:16.

It was not until years later that another scripture was revealed to me:

Jeremiah 29:11
For I know the thoughts that I think towards you, saith the Lord, thoughts of peace, and not of evil to give you an expected end.

So, who knew? God knew, and I still did not have a clue as to what God had planned for my life.

Chapter 2

THE UGLY
DUCKLING SYNDROME

"Once upon a time…" That's how I thought my life would start out. I loved reading fairy tales when I was younger because all of them had happy endings. But, oh, was I caught off guard when I realized life was no fairy tale.

The reality of life made me realize that in my tale, I didn't live in an enormous castle in the woods, there was no Prince Charming in shining armor riding a white stallion, and most importantly, I was not the beautiful princess.

In "Snow White and the Seven Dwarfs," the wicked witch says the famous line, "Mirror, mirror on the wall, who's the fairest one of all?" It was the mirror on the wall that fascinated me. That magic mirror always made me envious. If only I could have a magic mirror with the ability to transform myself into the fairest of them all. My moments in the mirror were spent questioning who I was. I would stand in front of the mirror and ask God, "Why did You make *me* ugly?"

I heard someone once say, "Don't get upset with the mirror, change the reflection."

The mirror only reveals what's being reflected; it's up to us to alter its appearance. But how? I was too young to understand all of the thoughts that were going through my mind.

Unfortunately, my home life was dysfunctional. I didn't have anyone that I could trust to talk about all of the thoughts running through my mind. I was afraid to talk about what I was dealing with at home and I did not know how to process my self-image issues. Escaping reality was easiest for me; I drifted off into my fairy tales and hid in the forest of my thoughts.

I felt comfortable thinking about the ugly duckling in my fantasy. Now that's a fairy tale I can relate to. Maybe, just maybe somewhere in the distant future, I could be pretty, accepted, and loved.

The story of the "The Ugly Duckling" was more reminiscent of my reality. Similar to the duckling, every young girl wants to feel loved, beautiful, and accepted–me included. As a young girl, my disposition was awkward, insecure, and introverted. My metal-rimmed glasses hung loosely from my head as it drooped in shame; I was embarrassed of my appearance. I was skinny as a rail, and going to school, my dresses were so long they all but dragged along the ground. For physical education class, my parents made me wear dresses instead of the normal PE shorts and t-shirt to exercise. I was teased because I didn't look like the other girls. While all the other girls were more stylish with their cute skirts and matching knee socks, my parents were "born-again" Christian believers, so "saved" that they used conservative attire as a badge of honor and a distinction from non-believers.

Buying friendship was how I thought friends were made; I felt as though I needed to make people like me. Unaware of my low self-esteem, I purchased lunches for classmates, bought gifts for "friends," gave away my own cherished possessions to whoever asked, and did whatever else it took to be accepted by the crowd.

Unfortunately, people began taking advantage of me. They really didn't want me to be a part of the group, they just wanted what I had to give them.

I didn't realize I was starving for attention and acceptance.

This ugly duckling from the fairy tales was dealing with low self-esteem because she didn't know who she was. She was in a place, but out of place. She was being made fun of because she didn't look like everyone else. Wow, that sounds just like me!

I felt ugly and incomplete, smiling on the outside, but screaming for help on the inside. I was introverted and held my head down because looking up only revealed an ugly person with no beauty to be seen.

I perceived God was punishing me through my parents' salvation and sanctified lifestyle. Now, I understand the blessing in having God-fearing parents; however, in my adolescent mind, it didn't make much sense.

At that time, I wasn't mature enough to know which questions to ask that would help me grow as a woman. I simply dealt with the hand I was given. That's how I was taught to process life's experiences. Why wasn't anyone there for me that I could share my secrets with, someone who believed in me? I didn't know how to express why I felt ugly, I just knew I was. No one knew what was causing me such pain and why I was unable to express my emotions. I later learned the pain and fear of my reality is what forced me to mentally and emotionally hit the escape button on life.

The right questions were:

- What is making me feel ugly?
- What was the cause of my pain?
- Why wasn't I able to express how I felt?
- What brought on such fear?
- Why would I want to hide in a fairy tale?

The fairy tale gave me a safe place, a peaceful place of no hurts, discriminations, or judgement. If I knew then what I know now, I would have been able to express the contempt I felt after having been robbed of my innocence.

Although it's painful to talk about my past, it's also a release for me to totally forgive and allow the Lord to heal me completely from the inside out.

Raised up in church, children had to stay in a child's place. We weren't allowed to ask many questions when it came to the decisions our parents made.

I didn't get many whippings, but the ones I did get were unforgettable! My mother would always say to me, "And this one is for the times you got by when I *should* have whipped you."

And, of course, the all-time favorite, "This is hurting me more than it's hurting you. You'll thank me later." Now, that statement I could never understand. How is my getting the whipping hurting you? No way am I going to thank you later.

It wasn't until I became of age that I realized that I was associating with ducks whose personalities did not fit in with what I was experiencing. Ducks quacked and made noise while I hardly made a sound. I just wanted to spread my wings and soar. I wanted to be someone else, but my environment, surroundings, and associations were holding me back and limiting my perception of who I was.

It wasn't until I had married, gone through a divorce, and raised a son when I met someone who told me that as long as I didn't like myself, I would always have low self-esteem. Their interest in me gave me hope. Somebody liked me for me. They helped select clothes that would make me feel good about myself. They kept telling me to hold my head up and stop doubting myself until, eventually, I finally got the message. I am fearfully and wonderfully made in God's image and that makes me unique.

I thank God for the season in which he brought that person into my life. I was constantly being reminded that I don't have to be that ugly duckling; I've been created to soar with the eagles, and that changed my way of thinking.

Chapter 3

NOT TONIGHT, I HAVE
A HEADACHE

I'm sure you have heard the statement, "Not tonight, dear; I have a headache."

You may even have been guilty of saying it yourself. It's the most widely known excuse women (and some men) use when they don't want to submit themselves to their spouse.

Somehow, that's the same way we treat God when we make excuses concerning why we are not doing the assignment He has given us.

The Bible speaks about all of the excuses people make as to why those invited could not or would not come to the supper.

Luke 14:16-20 reveals this parable:

> *Then said he unto him, A certain man made a great supper and bade many: And sent his servant at the supper time to say to them that were bidden, Come; for all things are now ready. And they all with one consent began to make excuse. The first said unto him, I have bought a piece of ground, and I must needs go and see it: I pray thee have me excused. And another said, I have bought five yoke of oxen, and I go to prove them: I*

*pray thee, have me excused. And another said, I have married
a wife, and therefore I cannot come.*

Can you imagine how this man felt after preparing a great feast
for his friends and they all had excuses?

The first invited guest allowed possessions to keep him from
attending the supper. The second guest allowed his business ven-
ture to stop him. Finally, the third allowed his natural affections to
keep him away.

Jesus used this parable to show how men and women make
excuses not to accept Him as their Lord and Savior, but I will take
it a little farther and include our reasons when God chooses us for a
specific work.

Your excuse may not be the same as mine, but it is still an excuse.

I used my insecurities as an excuse. I'm not eloquent in speech,
I don't know the Scriptures like other evangelists, and people who
know me probably won't listen to me. Just one excuse after another
made me very fearful and hesitant to move forward.

I didn't say "no" to the Lord, but actions (or no actions) speak
louder than words.

I used my family, my job, and my broken past as an excuse. I was
walking in condemnation and not in the Spirit.

Romans 8:1 declares, *There is therefore now no condemnation to
them which are in Christ Jesus, who walk not after the flesh, but after
the Spirit.*

The spirit of intimidation took over as I watched others go forth
with power and anointing. I envied them and wished I could do
what they did.

It took me a while to realize that I must work the works that He sent me to do. In other words, go into the vineyard and work.

Don't try to be like anyone else but Jesus. Being something or someone you're not will destroy you.

The Word tells us that we are without excuse. Christ died for all of them.

As I began studying more of the Word of God, I regained my assurance that God was in control of my destiny, that I was unique and not to be a carbon copy of someone else.

Learn from your past and don't allow your past to dictate your future. Saying "no" is not an option when it comes to the work of the Lord. Whether your no is verbal or in your actions, God knows what is best for you and me, and He never makes a mistake. The things we experience in life will either be a blessing or a lesson.

Chapter 4

FEAR FACTOR

Fear has a way of controlling your every move. The Bible says, "perfect love casts out all fear and fear has torment" (1 John 4:18). It was the torment that got to me.

I think that my fear stems from being rejected and disappointed so many times in my life; it was almost impossible for me to see it any other way.

My fears consumed me to the point that even knowing what the Word of God said, my fears spoke louder in my ears. My heart would pound and skip beats because I was so afraid. What was I so fearful of? I had so many shortcomings that I didn't think I could be effective in ministry. I was dealing with physical challenges, emotional challenges, and just all of the challenges that life brings.

My biggest fear was of people. What would they say? What were their opinions of me? Was it negative feedback or put downs? Were they laughing behind my back?

I found out that the mind can play some horrible tricks on us. I began thinking of some crazy stuff. Just envisioning people glaring and staring, making fun, or snickering and giggling at me made me cringe. People can be so judgmental, rude, crude, and unforgiving.

People won't let you forget your past. They'll say things like, "Isn't that the same person that...?" or "Wasn't she the one who...?" The list goes on and on. I just couldn't get pass that chatter.

I recently heard a statement that encouraged me. "People may know your past, but they don't know your future."

Fear had me so bound I felt chained to the past. It was hopeless for me. I decided that God really made a mistake because He wasn't helping me get over this fear. I felt crushed and helpless, but most of all, I failed God... again.

What do I do now? With no one to confide in, my only recourse was to talk to God. Guess what? That's where He wanted me to be... again.

Chapter 5

THE THREAT IS REAL

K now one thing; the devil does not like you. He hates you and what you stand for. The Word of God declares that he goes around like a roaring lion seeking whoever he may devour. He comes to steal, kill, and destroy… and he has you in mind.

It seemed the very moment I said "yes" to the will of God, the Enemy began working against me. When I realized the strategy he was using on me, I began to seek God in how to destroy the works of the devil and let his strategy backfire in his face.

God's Word tells us that the weapons of our warfare are not carnal; they are not human-made weapons (2 Corinthians 10:4). You cannot fight the Enemy with knives and guns. He is a spirit, and he only responds to the Word of God.

When Satan tried to entice Jesus on the mountain, he was shot down with, "It is written" (Matthew 4:1-11).

I realized early in ministry that you must know the Word of God for yourself.

One of my early experiences in knowing the Word of God and reading it for myself is when I wanted to accept the call. But I kept hearing, "How can *he* preach except *he* is sent?" I knew I wasn't a *he*, so how could I fulfill the call?

As I began to question the call, I wanted an answer from God, but I didn't want to go against what the preacher said.

There is not a time you ask God when He won't answer you back.

God spoke to me through the preached Word and out of nowhere, they said, "Read the Word for yourself. Don't just take my word for it."

I went home and began studying the Word and found a scripture that says, "How can they preach, except they are sent?" (Romans 10:15). What an insight into the Word! It was there all the time; I just failed to read it.

The Enemy will do anything and everything he can to stop you from doing the Lord's work. I've had to face sickness, death, depression, disappointments, you name it, and I've experienced it. The threat is real. Satan is not playing with us. His job is to destroy your testimony.

As I began to study Lucifer being cast out of heaven along with one-third of the angelic host, I couldn't imagine him giving up covering the throne of God and convincing so many of God's angels to follow him.

I realize that his fight is with God, and he uses us to get to God. His attack is real, but his focus is to show God that the creation he made was a mistake.

I understand more clearly, now more than ever, and I will not be a tool for the devil.

I bind every contrary spirit and every evil spirit. I bring my body under subjection, and I am experiencing transformation by the renewing of my mind.

Whoever said that a mind is a terrible thing to waste hit the nail on the head.

For me to act upon a thing, I must first conceive it in my mind, and then act upon what I was thinking.

If I think that I am defeated, all of my actions and speech will be that of defeat. But if I choose to think of things that are lovely, pure, and of a good report, my actions will respond accordingly.

That's where the Enemy gets many of us. We allow him to enter our ear gates and enter our minds. We then entertain those thoughts, and the Enemy say, "Gotcha."

Satan does not have dominion over me. I take authority over all of his works. He may be a threat, but he does not have the final say in Jesus's name. Amen!

Chapter 6

SHHH! I'VE GOT A SECRET

As children, we had many secrets, most of them were not that important, life changing, or even worth remembering as an adult.

It's the family secrets that haunt us; the skeletons in the closet, the ghosts in the attic, and the demons in the basement.

This is the part that really scares me because I've been ashamed of my past all of these years, but I felt it was necessary to share with you what I had experienced.

Abuse is a terrible thing; whether verbal, mental or physical, its effects are horrendous. You'll either become an introvert or go overboard as an extrovert. Being violated as a child can have horrific consequences.

As for me, I pushed my abuse so far in the back of my mind that I almost forgot about it. It was easier to pretend that it didn't happen, especially not in my family. How does one cope with this? Would anyone believe me if I told them? Will God ever forgive me or am I too tainted to be used by Him?

What would the church think of me? What would my friends think of me? How could I convince them it was not my fault, or maybe it was my fault?

Family is supposed to protect you, keep you from the evils of this world; you don't expect them to be participants of that evil.

Whether it's your mother, father, sister, brother, uncle, or cousin, it doesn't matter; they have a responsibility to protect you, not abuse you, right?

So, where was my safe place? Where could I run to find solace? I had no one to confide in, no one I could trust to share this with without being judged. I felt my life was ruined with no future and no hope.

Every message I heard, I felt ashamed. When the altar call was made during a service about abuse, I was too embarrassed to admit I was the one who had been abused. I didn't want people looking at me and whispering. You know how people can be sometimes. My pain was real and I was good at hiding it.

Year after year, I fought the thoughts that entered my mind. I even wanted to hate the people who violated me. I thought that if I could only get back at them for what they did, I would feel better, but feeling better never came.

I would pray and ask God to help me get over this, but every time I heard about someone being violated or abused, I would get angry. I never came to the point where I felt I could tell anyone what happened to me.

The interesting part of this entire experience, I've even counseled people who have been abused and helped them through their pain, but I could not trust anyone to help me through mine.

So, to share with you is a big part of my healing. It is important to me to let you know that no matter what you experienced in the past, it does not define your future.

I finally realized that God has my life in His hands, and nothing takes Him by surprise. He already knew and provided a way of escape.

Chapter 7

FIRE IN THE YES

How many times have we said "yes" to the Lord? When we hear a good message, "Yes, Lord" is our response. After we sing a good song, we say, "Yes, Lord, I'm available to You." As for me, I really believe I meant it at the time, but somehow I just didn't follow through on the "yes."

It sounds easy, but when I was put to the test, "yes" was not my first option. As a matter of fact, "yes" wasn't even in the equation. I avoided the call on my life for so long until I ultimately began to doubt it. I had the dreams, I had the prophecies, and at times, I actually walked in my calling, but I would never admit to it.

It was much easier *bootlegging*; I did the work, but I didn't want the responsibility of being called a missionary or evangelist. That called for separation, suffering, being talked about, and denial of friends and family. I wasn't ready for that.

Growing up in the church, I've seen too many people in ministry getting talked about, made fun of, and even hated for telling the truth. It seemed as though the more they preached, the worse things got for them. I couldn't understand why God would anoint someone and then allow him or her to experience tragedy, disappointment, sorrow, and pain.

It's okay to say yes, but let's be real, I am not the one to be persecuted and put down trying to minister to people who were just like me. I thought, who wants to hear me, anyway? My life has been so ragged and wretched. What could I possibly say? I failed in my first marriage, it was a total sham, and I had one of those shotgun weddings because I was pregnant.

My parents were avid workers in one of the largest churches in the city. I tried covering it up with marrying someone who I thought could take me from under the umbrella of my parents. I could live my own life, in my own house, with my own husband and child. Oh my, was I ever so disillusioned.

I was looking for that fairy tale ending. Instead, what I got was a nightmare on Elm Street.

I've always wondered why God allowed me to go through that experience, married to a man who lied his way through everything. I should have known something when we went to the court house to get the marriage license. He had lied about his age and had to go home, bring his birth certificate to validate his age, and his mother had to sign for him.

"Yes" seemed impossible for me. I could never be consistent. I became frustrated with my life; I felt I had no one to go to for direction. The friend I thought I had betrayed me, so that created a wall between me and people.

Never again would I share my feelings and have them exposed to the world.

Have you ever been in a revival or a service that was so powerful, and the Word of God came with such conviction that you just knew your life would change? And when the revival was over, you felt good that first week. You were inspired, motivated, charged up, and ready to do a work for the Lord.

Then the reality of life sets in, circumstances distracts you from your purpose and there you are back at the beginning… again. After going through those changes for so long, you're almost ready to give up, throw in the towel, and admit God made a mistake. "I can't be the one He wants to use because my life is a wretched mess." Well, I've been there.

I heard someone say recently that God knew you before the foundation of the world and nothing takes Him by surprise. God was aware that I was going to make some serious mistakes, bad decisions, and dumb choices, but He chose me anyway. It's because of these mistakes, bad decisions, and dumb choices that I now have a testimony. He knows the end from the beginning; it was just a matter of me filling in the blanks.

I think my problem was looking at other women in ministry. I wanted to preach like the ones who spoke powerful messages, or I wanted to sound and sing like others with beautiful voices. How did they get that revelation out of the same scripture I read? Did I just not see what they saw?

My main problem was comparing myself to others and feeling the need to be validated. My favorite phrases to use were "I can't," "I'm not good enough," "I don't have the charisma," and "I don't have the voice or volume." I was my biggest hindrance. Besides, it was an excuse that I could live with.

God understands me; He'll just get someone else. I was not comfortable in my own skin. So, I allowed those doubts and self-esteem issues to creep back in.

What would I do, where would I go, and who would I talk to? I felt like I was losing my mind. I had said, "yes," but it didn't seem to work for me. What was I doing wrong? God, please help me! And you know what? That's just the place where God wanted me to be.

Chapter 8

AGAINST ALL ODDS

At some point in your life, you have to take a stand. Either you're going to obey God's will or else face the consequences. Excuses won't seem to work anymore, there will be too many sleepless nights, and nothing will seem to go right.

Everything will seem to be taking off just fine, then for some reason you crash and burn. You ask yourself, "What happened? I thought I was making headway."

I got tired of the crash landings, being up and down, in and out. Like the prodigal son, I was in a pig pen feeding slop to the swine. What was I doing here?

I had to stop and look at me. What was disobedience doing to me? I wasn't happy. It appeared I was, but the reality of it all was just a façade, a false face. It was time to take the mask off.

Hiding the real me was my comfort zone. Nothing could reach me. I didn't have to face the realities of life.

But, how long could I hide from myself?

I began to pray to God and seek Him for direction, *clear* direction.

Even though I knew God had called me into ministry, I wanted to be sure without a shadow of doubt that this was His will for my life, and not just what someone told me or prophesized to me.

As I began to seek God and study His Word, I stopped looking to people and listening to negative responses. I began to see what God had chosen for me to do. God began sending others to encourage me and pray with me. Paul said, "Forgetting those things which are behind, press towards the mark" (Philippians 3:13). Sometimes you are pressing against all of the odds, but if God is for us, who can be against us?

I realize that I am not just a conqueror, but more than a conqueror through Jesus Christ. I can do all things through Christ that strengthens me.

With that in mind, I began to exercise my gift a little at a time. The Word of God declares, *gifts can open many doors and help you meet important people* (Proverbs 18:16 ERV).

God allowed us to put together a group of young women known as the Missionettes. We would come together to study the Word of God and minister at the various churches in the city.

Women in ministry did not have the freedom that we have now. We were not allowed in the pulpit, but could minister only from the floor. That was just fine with me because that brought us closer to the people! God began to save, heal, deliver, and set free.

I remember teaching my first lesson. It was on love.

> *Herein is our love made perfect, that we may have boldness in*
> *the day of judgment: because as he is so are we in this world.*
> 1 John 4:17

I was so nervous that my knees were knocking so loud I thought I was going to drop to the floor.

But as I took my eyes off of the people and began to focus on the Word that God had placed in my spirit, something awesome happened. Not only were the people of God blessed, but I was free from bondage. There was a release in my spirit and the chains of fear began to fall. Hallelujah, this was where I belonged! God placed compassion in my heart for His people. Not only to heal those who are bruised and wounded and not let them die, but to give them a healing balm to bind up their wounds and return them to the battlefields as victors and not victims.

I learned that the best testimony comes out of your own life experiences where people can relate. If God brought me out, He surely can bring you out.

It had not always been easy, but I remember an old song we used to sing that said, "It takes a well-made up mind to serve the Lord."

Once your mind is completely made up, nothing and no one can change it but you.

Chapter 9

THE HURT, THE HEALING, THE HOPE

THE HURT

> Isaiah 41:10
>
> *Fear not, for I am with you; be not dismayed, for I am your*
> *God, I will strengthen you, I will help you, I will uphold you*
> *with my righteous right hand.*

In losing a loved one, you know how painful and potent grief can be. Unfortunately, life is unpredictable, which means sorrow and death can come at any time. There's no way for us to prepare for this, but no matter how much we try to remember that our loved ones have moved on to a better place, we still mourn.

Have you ever been in a place where grief caught you by surprise? Things were out of your control, there were no immediate answers, and there was no one to turn to who would understand your plight? Life just seems like a roller coaster with ups, downs, turns, and spins.

Sometimes you feel you're at your breaking point, but God in His infinite wisdom intervenes on your behalf.

These last few months have been a whirlwind of challenges. It all began on my seventy-fifth birthday. Because of the COVID-19 pandemic, the family had to make changes in their plans to celebrate my special day. It ended up as a drive-by wave and say, "Happy Birthday!" My daughters, Karen and Ola, prepared a delicious dinner and the day went well. Everything seemed okay...

As Les and I returned home, we talked about celebrating our fiftieth wedding anniversary coming up the following year, February 6, and even decided on getting a brand-new automobile. Excitement was in the air; I couldn't stop smiling and grinning.

Later, that evening, Les told me that he didn't feel like himself and was going to turn in early. I asked if he wanted me to drive him to emergency care, and he replied, "No, I'll be alright." My next move was to call the family and they immediately called 911.

From that very first call, my life was changed forever. After 911 made their arrival, they determined that it was in the best interests of the patient to be sent to the nearest hospital for further examination. And because of COVID-19, I was unable to go with him. After a few hours of examination, Les was discharged from the hospital and returned home.

Within a couple of days, we had to call 911 again; this time, he has unable to use his left arm and was dragging his left leg. At this point, I knew there was something going on in his body that was not functioning properly. Again, I was not allowed to go with him to the hospital. After keeping him overnight in the hallway of the hospital to which he was sent, they released him, but without any communication from the doctor in charge as to what had happened.

At this time, I called to speak with his primary physician and was informed that he was on vacation.

After bringing Les home, it was apparent that he was not improving, but was getting worse.

He had lost all of his mobility and was bedridden. My family was incredibly supportive in taking care of their dad, even if it meant leaving their jobs and giving him full-time care.

Les's speech then became garbled, so much so that we could not understand what he was trying to tell us. I made one more 911 call, and once more, I was not able to go along with him in the ambulance or the hospital.

This time, though, I was permitted to stay in the parking lot of the hospital and speak with the on-duty doctor who informed me that Les was on life support, as he was no longer breathing on his own, and he had been given a gastrostomy tube to get some nourishment into his system. I was told then that Les had a massive brain stroke and his survival was determined to be just a few minutes.

I was stunned. I couldn't find the words to say. I was paralyzed for a moment; my heart began beating so fast, and my mind was in a fog. I almost lost consciousness.

My daughter, Karen, and my son, Les, Jr., were able to go into ICU to be with him. I could only watch via FaceTime. After hearing all of what was keeping him alive, even then, there was little hope. I asked Karen and Les Jr. their opinion of their dad's survival. Their opinion along with the doctor on duty in the ICU was that his condition was determined to be grave. I asked Karen to put the phone to his ear and as I talked to him and prayed, I told him that I was releasing him into the presence of the Lord. It took great strength to say good-bye.

The next few days, I was so disoriented, so lost for words, trying to go through my mind if there was anything more I could have done. The love of my life for fifty years was no longer there with me. He would never walk in our house again. There would be no more conversations, no more laughs, no more dreams, no more Hawaiian vacations.

I had questions to ask God, but I couldn't put them into words. Lord, what am I supposed to do now? Where do I start? How do I go on from here? My heart was aching, my spirit was broken, my life was in shambles. God and Les were the only ones I could count on to talk about my feelings, my turmoil, my achievements, and my failures.

I know everyone grieves in their own way, but no matter who you have lost or how you cope, it will take time to heal. During the most painful moments, it's important to turn to friends, family, and faith for support. God will forever be by our side to comfort us, make us hopeful once again, and give us guidance during the good times and the bad times. The best Bible verses for coping with death might just make you feel less alone. Grief may feel like it's never-ending, but listening to God's Word allows you to feel your emotions and not try to hide them. And giving yourself time to process all that you have been through, you will soon find comfort again.

I've been hurt before, but I've never felt pain like this. It was taking me into despair and depression.

Scripture is a path to personal revelation. Then, I remembered the Words of the Lord, Isaiah 41:10 (ESV):

> Fear not, for I am with you' be not dismayed, for I am your God, I will strengthen you, I will help you, I will uphold you with my righteous hand.

THE HEALING

Isaiah 53:3

He is despised and rejected of men; a man of sorrows, and acquainted with grief: and we hid as it were our faces from him; he was despised, and we esteemed him not.

Revelation 21:4

And God shall wipe away all tears from their eyes; and there shall be no more death, neither sorrow, nor crying, neither shall there be any more pain: for the former things are passed away.

The truth is that we never get over the people we lose, but it's understandable that finding ways to move forward in our lives and be here without the people we love can feel daunting, destressing, frightening, and intimidating when you are going through a big loss.

But how do we heal from our loss? My family was there and is still there to help me get through my grief. Even though I had read scripture after scripture, it was not quickly registering.

My pastor administrative assistant Jeffrey M. Lewis walked me through my grief by being compassionate in asking me to return to the weekly church Bible study session Wednesday In The Word as a teacher.

After giving some thought, I agreed and, immediately, I was given dates to minister.

This was a part of my healing because I was constantly reading, researching, and studying God's Word. I was so engrossed in ministering to God's people, I began to sense a release.

My family began to say things that their dad would do or say that would make us laugh. And we're still laughing today.

My close friend reminded me of the funny thing that Les would ask of me. She reminded me that he always wanted string beans and cranberry sauce with his meals. I had to buy string beans and cranberry sauce by the case!

I still have my private moments of tears, but God always wipes them away.

I've listed some information that may help you get through your **hurt to healing**. First is an article I found on the University of Rochester Medical Center Health Encyclopedia about healing from loss.

Grief and Loss: The Process of Healing

Losing a loved one is one of the most difficult events you can experience. Understanding grief and learning how to cope can help you heal and move forward with your life as you honor the person you miss.

Q. What is grief?
A. Grief is what you feel when you lose someone or something dear to you. How long you grieve depends on the closeness of the relationship. Whether the death was sudden or expected, the nature of the bond also affects how long you grieve.

When you grieve, you often have intense and enduring feelings of disbelief, shock, despair, sadness, and guilt that can be hard to deal with. Even so, these feelings are a normal part of the healing process. Experiencing them will allow you to move on with your life.

Q. What can help me heal from grief and loss?
A. Support from others is one of the most important parts in healing. That support can come from:

- *Close friends*
- *Grief counselors and social workers*
- *Grief support groups*
- *Other family members*
- *Psychotherapists*
- *Your faith community*

Q. What self-care steps or coping skills do I need?
A. It's important to take care of yourself. You should try to do the following:

- *Eat a healthy diet.*
- *Exercise regularly.*
- *Get enough sleep.*
- *Maintain your normal routine.*

Resist the urge to numb the pain with alcohol or drugs. This can delay healing and lead to further problems.

Some people also find creating a meaningful memorial in the person's honor to be helpful. For example, fund a scholarship program or give a gift to a charity or aid fund in the person's name.

Finally, be patient with yourself. There's no universal timetable for grief.

Q. What role does mourning play?
A. Mourning is the public side of grief and varies from culture to culture. Regardless of the ritual, mourning provides an accepted way to recognize the death of a loved one. It also helps you say goodbye in a public ceremony that honors the person. It gives family members ongoing support and sympathy.

Q. When should I seek professional help?
A. While grief is similar to depression, clinical depression is a psychological disorder. Grief is a normal response to loss. But grief can lead to depression.

Contact your healthcare provider right away if you have any of the following:

+ Your symptoms last for more than 1 year after a major event.
+ You resort to drugs or alcohol. Call 911 if you have thoughts of suicide.[1]

Here is another article about traveling along the road of grief from New Church.

---

[1] "Grief and Loss: The Process of Healing," University of Rochester Medical Center Health Encyclopedia, medically reviewed by L Renee Watson MSN RN, Raymon Turley Jr. PA-C, and Steven Buslovich MD, https://www.urmc.rochester.edu/encyclopedia/content.aspx?contenttypeid=1&contentid=4287.

Grief is a person's spiritual, emotional, intellectual and physical reaction to loss, which can begin before the loss actually occurs and persists until the grief reaction is no longer noticed. People in the helping professions know that a person's experience of grief is short or long, mild or disruptive, mental or physical, depending on both obvious and subtle influences. You have experienced grief. Perhaps a favorite piece of clothing wore out, you moved away from friends, or a parent died. Perhaps you experienced panic, or depression, or despair, or sadness, or nostalgia, or anger, or something else. Maybe you experienced foggy thinking, an absence of emotions, uncontrolled emotions, a loss of appetite, joint pain, or any number of other sensations.

Your experience of grief will be unique, even though it may include states others experience. That you experience your own grief is wonderful, actually, because the Lord is accommodating His divine love and wisdom to you in a way specific to your spiritual and physical needs. This is the first observation from New Church ideas that can help you. The Lord actively leads you through a process which is governed by His rules of love. This will progress to completion, and He will return you to a balanced state in which you can again experience joy.

As the New Church teaches, love creates and maintains a spiritual connection; *the tighter the connection, the more the loss affects us and impacts our spiritual and natural worlds.*

Perhaps you have experienced a sudden loss: a pet died accidentally, or you were fired without warning. The experience shocks you, spiritually and physically, disrupting thought and even movement. These effects of the shock of the loss are so significant that researchers found they can be measured in the brain. Perhaps the Lord wants you to stop everything for a moment rather than do something damaging to your process of recovery. Typically, a grieving person either does almost nothing for some time, or merely "goes through the motions" on emotional autopilot. During this static stage, your identity is protected, allowing you to continue through the process without requiring permanent changes to your personality in order to cope. The Lord preserves your eternal welfare, even though you have lost something integral to your spiritual life.

Grieving includes using coping mechanisms to deal with your loss. Not everyone cries, but everyone needs the sphere of love around them. Like many, you may turn inward, reflecting on a picture bigger than you have ever considered before. The Word explains that this happens because what is mortal is put right next to what you want to be immortal in your mind and heart. You sense your own mortality as a new reality. If you experience sudden loss, you may feel a new fear of the future—a worry that you could die tomorrow. You may feel anxiety that you have not become a good person or that you have not achieved your life's goals.

This tension creates an emotional rollercoaster that comes from resisting the Lord's care, His providence, which leaves us unsatisfied and weary. *The ride only slows and levels out as you acknowledge the reality of the loss and give yourself permission to experience sadness, loneliness or helplessness. Your intellect may find it hard to believe, but the fact is that when you let go and grieve—an act of will—you let God carry you through the process to the end of the ride, when you can walk on your own in the joy of being on solid ground.*

Many who grieve notice that the story of the loss runs around in their minds in bits and pieces. Perhaps you have experienced this. Some of the bits are accurate memories of what happened, and you can feel badly, even responsible, for the loss. Some of the memories are inaccurate and cause you unnecessary distress. One way to discover the difference, and to be able to put the story "to bed," is to tell the story. Of course, there will be more analysis, and perhaps regrets and resentment. But when these are put in the context of your eternal life and the eternal life of your loved one (if that is what you are grieving), the Lord puts the pieces together in a way that helps you overcome any distress. Given time and cooperation, the Lord will finish the puzzle of your life, and you can enjoy a whole picture.[2]

HOPE

Corinthians 15:19

If in this life only we have hope in Christ, we are of all men most miserable.

Psalm 31:24

Be of good courage, and he shall strengthen your heart, all ye that hope in the Lord.

Psalm 16:9

Therefore my heart is glad, and my glory rejoiceth: my flesh also shall rest in hope.

---

[2] Reverend Clark Echols, "The journey of grief," *New Church Connection 2010 Issue 2: Grief and Acceptance*, Glendale New Church, https://newchurch.org/get-answers/connection-magazine/grief-and-acceptance/the-journey-of-grief/.

Titus 2:13

*Looking for that blessed hope, and the glorious appearing of
the great God and our Saviour Jesus Christ;*

There *is* hope after grief.

How does one describe *hope after the loss of someone you love?* Without
Christ, there is no hope. Without Christ, life would be hopeless.

Titus 2:13

*Looking for that blessed hope, and the glorious appearing of
the great God and our Savior Jesus Christ;*

This blessed hope when we are taken to be with Jesus at the resur-
rection of the dead—the rapture of the church—is a right and a privi-
lege that is given for *all* who are saved by grace through faith in Christ.
And when He appears, "we shall be like Him for we shall see Him as
He is" (1 John 3:2).

We have hope that we will see our loved ones again. God shall
wipe all tears from our eyes. No more sadness and grief.

After our loss of a loved one, we may try to hide our feelings
by putting on a smile. We may also constantly give that automatic
response of "I'm fine" anytime someone asks how we're doing. On
the other hand, if we're watching someone grieve, our hearts long for
them to be happy again. But if we push too hard for their happiness,
it may reduce their ability to grieve as needed. As much as we may
hate it, grief is a part of life.

Ecclesiastes 3:1-4

To every thing there is a season, and a time to every purpose under the heaven: A time to be born, and a time to die; a time to plant, and a time to pluck up that which is planted; A time to kill, and a time to heal; a time to break down, and a time to build up; A time to weep, and a time to laugh; a time to mourn, and a time to dance;

Yes, we will experience grief in this lifetime. God's Word not only gives us permission to grieve, but also promises comfort and hope as we endure it.

In the Gospel of John, we find a well-known, easily quoted verse "Jesus wept" (John 11:35). While it's the shortest verse in all of Scripture, this two-word passage is packed full of significance. In this story, Jesus returns to the home of Mary and Martha after the death of their brother, His friend Lazarus. Upon seeing Mary weeping, His heart broke with hers as He began to weep, as well.

If Jesus wept over His lost loved one, we know that it's okay for us to do the same. Even though His weeping was short-lived as Lazarus was raised back to life in the following verses, our Savior still found it necessary to grieve. Our grief may last a lot longer than those few moments Jesus endured, but His tears give us permission to shed as many tears as we need to.

The Lord is near to the broken-hearted and saves those who are crushed in spirit.

King David, the writer of this verse, was well-acquainted with grief. First, his best friend Jonathan died. Then his first child died. But during those times, he appeared to discover a comforting truth that

God gets close in those heart-breaking seasons. And His immediate presence is exactly what we need in those moments.

Yes, there is hope after grief. I have found it and you can, too.

Chapter 10

I'm Here

I'm not supposed to be here… but God! I'm here by the grace of God! God knew the plans He had for me, even before the foundation of the earth. He chose me, despite my doubts, insecurities, fears, and failures. He had me covered with His hedge of protection, and endowed me with unmerited grace, mercy, and favor. Instead of the prospects of being consumed in eternal fire, by grace, I am overtaken and overshadowed by His holy fire. I'm not supposed to be here, but **I'm here**!

> Philippians 1:6
> *being confident of this, that **he** who began **a good work** in you*
> *will care it on to completion until the day of Christ Jesus.*

I challenge you; take the plunge and obey God. See if He won't come through for you. God does not love me any more than He loves you.

God promises in His Word that He would never leave you or forsake you. His Holy Spirit has given us power over the Enemy. "Greater is he that is in us than he that is in the world" (1 John 4:4).

I guarantee it will be a life-changing experience when you allow God to get the glory out of your life.

We have no more time to waste. Souls are waiting for you; deliverance is in your spirit. Yes! Stop running with the crowd and become a majority of one!

ABOUT THE AUTHOR

Evangelist Barbara Bean was born in North Carolina. Her family moved to Los Angeles, California where she completed her formal education.

She is the widow of the late Elder Leslie Bean as they shared a beautiful marriage that lasted nearly fifty years. They have five adult children: Kevin, Karen, Da'Niel, Ola and Les Jr.

Evangelist Bean was called to the ministry in April 1969 and has ministered on skid row, boy's camps, women's prison, convalescent homes, television, radio, in the Virgin Islands, Freeport Haiti, as well as locally. She is the founder and CEO of Outreach/Breakthrough Ministries, established in 1975. Evangelist Bean is totally involved in the music ministry, having served under Dr. Mattie Moss Clark, Dr. Judith McAllister, Elder Tony McGill, Evangelist Markita Knight, and Elder Donnell Wright State Minister of Music So. Cal. Jurisdiction 1. A song writer, director, writer, and producer of plays and concerts, she is dedicated to serving God and the community.

CPSIA information can be obtained
at www.ICGtesting.com
Printed in the USA
BVHW011714050423
661819BV00014B/236

9 781662 874284